Ed Reed

Martin Gitlin
AR B.L.: 7.0 Alt.: 1060
Points: 2.0   MG

SUPERSTARS

of
PRO FOOTBALL

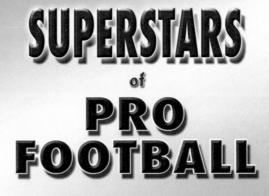

Martin Gitlin

Mason Crest Publishers

Produced by OTTN Publishing in association with
21st Century Publishing and Communications, Inc.

MASON CREST PUBLISHERS INC.
370 Reed Road
Broomall, Pennsylvania 19008
(866) MCP-BOOK (toll free)
www.masoncrest.com

Printed in the United States of America.

First Printing

9 8 7 6 5 4 3 2 1

Library of Congress Cataloging-in-Publication Data

Gitlin, Marty.
    Ed Reed / Martin Gitlin. — 1st printing.
        p. cm. — (Superstars of pro football)
    Includes bibliographical references.
    ISBN 978-1-4222-0558-7 (hardcover) — ISBN 978-1-4222-0834-2 (pbk.)
    1. Reed, Ed, 1978–   —Juvenile literature. 2. Football players—United States—Biography—Juvenile literature. I. Title.
GV939.R437G58 2008
796.332092—dc22
[B]   2008024184

Publisher's note:
All quotations in this book come from original sources, and contain the spelling and grammatical inconsistencies of the original text.

◀◀ **CROSS-CURRENTS** ▶▶

In the ebb and flow of the currents of life we are each influenced by many people, places, and events that we directly experience or have learned about. Throughout the chapters of this book you will come across **CROSS-CURRENTS** reference bubbles. These bubbles direct you to a **CROSS-CURRENTS** section in the back of the book that contains fascinating and informative sidebars and related pictures. Go on. ▶▶

CONTENTS

1 **Back in Hawaii Again** 4

2 **Planting the Seeds of Greatness** 10

3 **The Making of a Superstar** 16

4 **Better Player and Better Man** 26

5 **Generous Heart and Sure Hands** 36

Cross-Currents 46

Chronology 56

Accomplishments & Awards 57

Further Reading & Internet Resources 58

Glossary 59

Notes 61

Index 62

Picture Credits 64

About the Author 64

BACK IN HAWAII AGAIN

National Football League (NFL) players don't just work from the beginning of **training camp** until the season's end. They toil and sweat all year to be the best. At the end of the season, the best players are thankful to be chosen to play in the annual Pro Bowl game in Hawaii, a game reserved for the league's premier talent.

One would think that by 2008, Baltimore Ravens **safety** Ed Reed might have gotten used to this honor. After all, that year he was chosen to compete in the Pro Bowl for the fourth time. The thrill, however, had never worn off. Ed still felt a sense of excitement and achievement at earning a spot alongside the world's top players.

Baltimore Ravens safety Ed Reed is introduced as a member of the AFC's Pro Bowl team, February 2004. In his first six seasons in the NFL, Ed was invited to play in the annual all-star game four times.

A Special Year

Ed had been picked to play in the Pro Bowl for the **American Football Conference (AFC)** team after his second and third seasons in the National Football League. During the 2005 season, however, Ed suffered from something that most NFL players experience at least once in their careers—a serious injury.

Ed missed six games in 2005 because of an ankle injury. He was not voted into the Pro Bowl, which was held in February 2006. He knew his performance wasn't up to his usual standards that season. He didn't want to make excuses, even though it had been difficult to reach the level of excellence he had become used to.

CROSS-CURRENTS

Read "The Pro Bowl" if you'd like to learn more about the National Football League's annual all-star game. Go to page 46. ▶▶

The pain Ed felt in his heart that year matched the pain he felt in his ankle. He wanted so badly to play well again, but he understood that it would take time to recover. Ed placed a sheet of scrap paper containing a Bible verse in his locker. The verse served as a reminder to Ed to be patient, not just in his career, but also in his life. Ed explained what that little piece of paper meant to him:

> **"I have to be reminded by it always, but it's something that over time really built up just going through life situations. Relating to football, especially playing safety, I got a lot of [criticism] last year, kind of this year, too, because [I wasn't making big] plays."**

During the 2006 season, Ed put his injury behind him. He again performed as one of the best **defensive backs** in the NFL, just as he had earlier in his career. He started in all 16 games for the Ravens and recorded five **interceptions**, including one he ran back 25 yards for a touchdown. He registered 59 tackles and was named first-team **All-Pro** along with the other great players of the game.

Ed explained his belief that if he remained patient, his talent would allow him to raise his performance to its usual high level:

CROSS-CURRENTS

To learn about some other current top players at Ed's position, check out "A Safety Issue." Go to page 47. ▶▶

Ed (number 20) heads upfield after intercepting a pass during a 2006 game against the Pittsburgh Steelers. In 2006, Ed proved that he was fully recovered from an ankle injury that had slowed him during the previous season.

> **"**Football is that up-and-down type of game. It's not going to always come your way, but when it does, you've got to make the best of your opportunities.**"**

The Ravens certainly made the best of their opportunities as well. In 2006, they won 13 of 16 games and qualified for the **playoffs**.

It was no surprise that Ed was selected to play in the 2007 Pro Bowl. When he got to Hawaii, Ed soaked up the sunshine—and the knowledge that he was again considered one of the top players in football.

Thievery in Honolulu

Dallas Cowboys quarterback Tony Romo also received a lot of deserved attention in 2006, and he emerged as an NFL star. In the

An aerial view of Aloha Stadium in Honolulu, Hawaii, during the 2007 Pro Bowl pregame show. Ed picked off two passes during the game, helping the AFC team earn a 31-28 victory.

2007 Pro Bowl, Romo had the same experience as nearly all of his peers. He had a pass picked off by Ed Reed.

Ed's AFC team had taken an early lead in the game, and Ed was determined to prevent the **National Football Conference (NFC)** team from gaining points. The NFC team, however, had driven down the field and was on the verge of scoring a touchdown that would put it right back in the game.

Romo, the NFC quarterback, backpedaled and surveyed the AFC's defense. He was looking to throw the ball into the end zone. There was one problem, however, and that problem was Ed Reed. Ed intercepted the pass to stop the NFC's drive and keep the AFC well ahead.

It was just what Romo had been trying to guard against. Other quarterbacks who had been well aware of where Ed was on the field still ended up shaking their heads after he intercepted their passes. Ed had simply welcomed Romo into the large group of quarterbacks who had been victimized by his thievery.

After the game, Romo explained what had happened:

❝I didn't want to throw it up, because you have Ed Reed back there and you don't want him taking [it in for a touchdown].❞

That interception wasn't Ed's only theft of the day. He recorded another interception to tie the Pro Bowl record of two interceptions in one game. The accomplishment came as no surprise to anyone in the stadium that day, least of all Ed's fellow players. After all, Ed had been intercepting passes and frustrating quarterbacks from the moment he first stepped onto a football field. He had earned a reputation as an aggressive defensive back who was willing to take chances long before he first put on a Ravens jersey.

PLANTING THE SEEDS OF GREATNESS

Ed Reed didn't always display the good work ethic that allowed him to blossom into a football star. In his early youth, Ed was quite a poor student, not because he was incapable of performing better in the classroom, but because he had weak study habits and he lacked motivation. Ed's grades were well below average in school.

One day, however, Ed decided he no longer wanted to waste his potential. That's when he made an important decision. It was just before his junior year at Destrehan High School. The school is near his hometown of St. Rose, Louisiana, where Ed was born on September 11, 1978. Ed got up the nerve to ask Jeanne Hall, a secretary to the assistant principal, if he could move in with her family.

It's not that Ed didn't have loving parents. His mother and father, Karen and Ed Reed Sr., had raised and nurtured him up to that point. Ed loved and respected his mom and dad. Ed Reed Sr. was a hardworking ship welder and crane operator who rose every morning at 3 A.M. to go to work. He did not want his son to follow his career path.

Ed Sr. expressed his concerns to his son in no uncertain terms:

> **❝Son, you don't ever want to make a living doing what I do.❞**

CROSS-CURRENTS

If you want to learn more about Ed Reed's childhood hometown, read "All about St. Rose." Go to page 48. ▶▶

Ed Reed followed a challenging path to reach the NFL. As a young man growing up in Louisiana, he needed help to develop the discipline and good study habits required for success.

Ed Sr. wanted what was best for his son, whom he believed had the talent to play professional football. The Hall family had helped other troubled young people become more disciplined and focused. So the Reeds allowed Ed to move in with the Halls.

Changing A Life

Jeanne Hall believed Ed needed two things to thrive in school: a structured lifestyle and an improved attitude. She created a schedule in which Ed would eat and nap after football practice, then get up at 9:30 P.M. and study until midnight.

The Destrehan High School field house displaying the Fighting Wildcats logo. Ed was an exceptional athlete at Destrehan High School and lettered in football, basketball, baseball, and track and field. In addition to being an outstanding football player, Ed also won a state championship in the javelin throw.

Ed's grades rose dramatically, giving him confidence in his studies and in other areas of his life. Ed adopted a personal motto: Listen, learn, then lead. He explained how the Halls helped him reach his potential:

> **"There was something inside of me that [the Halls] brought out. And once I realized what I could do, I wanted to take it to another level. I saw if I did things right, people would follow me."**

While playing football, Ed had always been able to read situations and make the right decisions. After moving in with the Halls, he could do the same off the field.

A Maturing Young Man

On one occasion, Ed and two friends joined Jeanne and her three children for a night at the movies. The movie cashier, however, refused entrance to the three black teenagers. She explained that due to discipline problems they had been having at the theater, only children accompanied by a parent or guardian were allowed in.

Jeanne said that since she was such a close friend to the boys, she might as well be considered their family. The cashier still refused to let them in. Jeanne then began to argue with a police officer who had stepped in. As the discussion became more heated, Ed calmly suggested that they leave and rent a movie instead. The group took his advice and walked away.

Ed had shown an ability to size up trouble and end it peacefully. Meanwhile, he was giving quarterbacks and receivers nothing but trouble on the football field.

Ed Gets Ahead

The work ethic and attitude that made Ed a better student helped him excel in sports as well. He did not just play football at Destrehan High School. He was also a standout athlete in basketball, baseball, and track and field. Ed received several honors as a baseball pitcher. As a member of the track team, he won a state championship in the javelin throw.

In four seasons with the Miami Hurricanes, Ed established himself as an outstanding ball-hawk. As a senior in 2001, he intercepted nine passes to lead all college players. That year, Miami finished 12-0 and won the national championship.

It was his heroics in football, however, that brought the most attention. Ed grew into a major college prospect as a senior, when he recorded 83 tackles, seven interceptions, and three forced fumbles. He even ran three **punts** back for touchdowns that year. Ed was so valuable and versatile that Destrehan coach Scott Martin also used him on offense as a running back and a quarterback.

By that time, college **scouts** were hot on Ed's trail. He was **recruited** strongly by Louisiana State University and the University of Miami, along with many other schools. Ed chose to attend Miami, which had one of the top football programs in the country.

College Football Star

At Miami, Ed didn't disappoint anyone. He broke the school record with 21 interceptions during his career there. He also shattered other marks, gaining a total of 389 yards and scoring five touchdowns after interceptions. He helped the Hurricanes win a national championship in 2001.

It's no wonder that Ed earned **All-American** status in both his junior and senior years. *Football News* named him National Defensive Player of the Year after the 2001 season. For good measure, Ed continued his track and field career and won the Big East Conference championship in the javelin throw in 1999. Ed also set a Miami track and field team record in this event.

CROSS-CURRENTS

For some history about the college where Ed played football between 1997 and 2001, read "The Miami Hurricanes." Go to page 48. ▶▶

The only question to be answered after college was which NFL team would select him in the 2002 **draft**. That lucky team was the Ravens, who chose Ed with the 24th overall pick of the first round.

Many people believed he would be picked earlier, but Ed used the fact that he dropped to the 24th spot as motivation. He wanted to show the teams that passed him by that they had made a mistake in doing so—and that's exactly what he did.

THE MAKING OF A SUPERSTAR

Ed Reed was no speed demon coming out of college. He was not considered particularly quick or strong. At 5-foot-11, he was a bit shorter than what scouts felt was the ideal height for a defensive back, but Ed certainly made the teams that passed him by in the 2002 draft wish they hadn't.

Ed proved from the start of his NFL career that he was one heck of a football player. In fact, while other rookies hoped desperately just to make the team, Ed earned a spot as a starter. He would be a fixture as a Ravens safety for years to come.

An Immediate Impact

Generally, the eyes of a quarterback or receiver light up when

Ed kept his eye on the ball during his first season in the NFL. After being drafted by the Baltimore Ravens in 2002, Ed earned a starting spot. As a rookie, Ed picked off five passes.

they see a rookie playing defensive back for an opponent. These players believe they can take advantage of a first-year player. However, they quickly came to fear Ed Reed.

Ed didn't play like a rookie in 2002. Instead, he performed like a safety that had been roaming around NFL fields for quite a while. Many rookies are a little timid when they first compete at that level, but Ed proved quite the opposite. Starting with his first game, Ed earned a reputation as a ball-hawk who wasn't afraid to take chances.

In a late September game against Denver, Ed got on a roll and didn't stop. He grabbed his first career interception in that game and recorded the first blocked punt in the seven-year history of the Ravens franchise. He intercepted another pass in a victory over Cleveland the following week.

Ed was merely warming up. In an early November game against the Bengals, Ed intercepted two passes, the second of which clinched a Ravens victory. In a win two weeks later against the Tennessee Titans, Ed blocked another punt, scooped up the ball, and sprinted into the end zone for a key touchdown.

Ed ended the season as impressively as he began it, with a season-high 8 tackles in a game against Pittsburgh.

Working to Be the Best

Ed finished his first season fourth on the team with 85 tackles. He tied a team rookie record with five interceptions, and was among the NFL leaders in that category. Ed was a primary reason why the Ravens led the NFL with 25 interceptions in 2002. Ed also deflected 13 passes—nearly one a game.

By the end of the 2002 season, many coaches and players considered Ed to be one of the better safeties in the NFL. Ed, however, was not quite satisfied. After the year was over, Ed spoke about how much he wanted to improve in the future:

"I'm always thinking about football because it's in my heart. I want to be the best at my position across the league. I want to be the best ever at safety, so anytime people speak about safeties, I want them speaking of Ed Reed."

The Ravens play their home games at this stadium near the harbor in Baltimore. Ed fit right in with the Baltimore franchise, which by 2002 had become known for its tough defensive style of play.

One man who appreciated what Ed had achieved in his first season was Ravens **defensive coordinator** Mike Nolan. Nolan was pleasantly surprised at the young safety's knowledge of football and his ability to rise to the occasion when a game was on the line. Nolan explained:

❝[Ed's] a guy who loves the game, visualizes the game, and prepares while he's on and off the field. . . . He's an excellent football player who outplayed a lot of veterans.❞

CROSS-CURRENTS

To learn more about one of Ed's most famous teammates on the Ravens' defense, read "The Great Ray Lewis." Go to page 50. ▶▶

It was quickly becoming obvious that Ed was an intelligent player. He was a generous one as well—Ed bought his mother a fully furnished home in 2002 before he even purchased a house for himself.

Like a Seasoned Pro

Ed played well as a rookie, but he was sensational during his second season. In 2003 he strengthened his reputation as someone who could make a huge impact on a game with one great play.

One of those plays occurred in mid-September in a victory over Cleveland. Ed intercepted a pass and raced 54 yards for a touchdown

Ed dives for a loose ball during a 2003 game against Kansas City. That season, Ed intercepted seven passes and knocked down nine others. He returned one of his picks 54 yards to score his first NFL touchdown.

on the final play of the game. He had already registered another theft that day, which gave him two interceptions in a game for the second time in his professional career.

By that time, opposing quarterbacks were afraid Ed would pick off their passes, but they weren't the only ones concerned. Opposing offensive players were also worried about just how far Ed would run if he intercepted a pass. In the following week, during a game against San Diego, Ed recorded another long interception return, weaving his way 27 yards downfield.

Ed was becoming a first-class pest who was making a habit out of thievery. He picked off his fourth pass in just five games during a contest against the Arizona Cardinals, giving him the NFL lead in interceptions. There seemed to be no stopping him.

A Punt Player

Ed took pride not only in his work as a safety but also in his performance on punt coverage. Remarkably, he blocked the third punt of his young career during that same game against Arizona, and he returned it 22 yards for a touchdown. After that game, it came as no surprise that he was named AFC Special Teams Player of the Week.

When asked about the play, however, Ed answered in his usual modest way:

> **"After I [blocked the punt], I located [the ball] in the air and pretty much played it off the bounce and caught it. I just picked it up, and whatever happens after that, happens."**

Ed has never been one to boast about his ability. He has always preferred to show it on the field. Ed might not have said much about his performance, but Ravens coach Brian Billick wasn't about to let praise go unspoken:

> **"Spectacular player. He has a real knack for it."**

Playoff Territory

Ed continued to display that knack in helping Baltimore qualify for the NFL playoffs. In a game against Seattle, Ed blocked a punt and returned the ball 16 yards for a touchdown. This play launched the Ravens' comeback from a 17-point deficit.

By the time the regular season ended, Ed was tied for the NFL lead in interceptions, with seven. He was also ready for his first playoff game. Ed rose to the occasion, intercepting a pass against Tennessee, but the Ravens lost a close game, ending the team's season.

Ed, however, was recognized for his brilliant second year. He was selected as an All-Pro by *Sports Illustrated* and was named to the All-AFC Team by *Pro Football Weekly*. He received several other honors as well, including his first trip to the Pro Bowl—but the best was yet to come.

A Long Run

It was November 7, 2004, and well into Ed's third season. He already had achieved some spectacular feats that season, but he was about to outdo himself. The Ravens led 20-13 in a game against Cleveland, but the Browns were on the verge of scoring a game-tying touchdown.

Browns quarterback Jeff Garcia backpedaled to pass, but he was hit by Ravens **linebacker** Ray Lewis as he released the ball. The ball bounced off the shoulder of a Browns receiver in the end zone. Reacting quickly and instinctively, Ed snagged it for his fourth interception of the season.

Ed could have just kneeled down and let his team run out the clock for the victory, but instead, Ed ran. And ran. And ran. He ran until he had covered an incredible 106 yards for a touchdown. This set the record for the longest touchdown run after an interception in NFL history.

The play symbolized Ed's amazing season. As usual, Ed refused to brag. Instead, he spoke about his passion for football and how he enjoyed helping his team:

> **❝It's really just exciting for me to go out and play the game, to get up on another Sunday and have the same kind of fun you've been having since you were a kid. . . . To know that I can make a play, or maybe even win the game, that's exciting to me.❞**

Nobody Better in 2004

Ed apparently enjoyed intercepting passes in the end zone, because he did it again the following week in a game against the New York

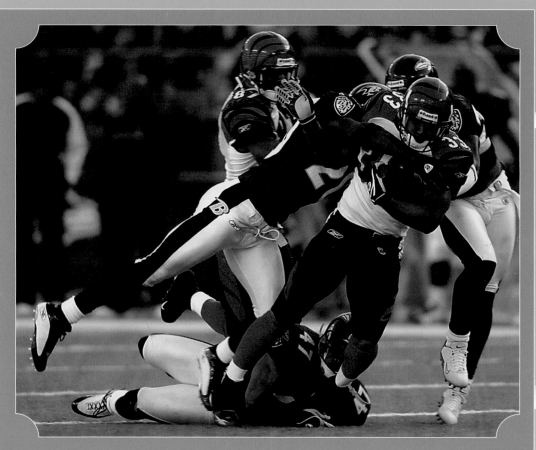

During a 2004 game, Ed hauls down Cincinnati running back Kenny Watson (number 33). Ed's ferocious tackling forced three fumbles in 2004. He also led the NFL with nine interceptions that season.

Jets. This time Ed sprinted 78 yards to set up the Ravens' first touchdown of the game. Such amazing plays motivated the NFL to select Ed as the AFC Defensive Player of the Month for November 2004.

Ed didn't just make plays covering receivers. The Ravens also used his talent to surprise quarterbacks dropping back to pass. On one occasion, Ed stunned Washington Redskins quarterback Mark Brunell by chasing him 15 yards, tackling him, and stripping the ball away. He then scooped it up and ran 22 yards for a touchdown.

By that time Ed had secured a reputation as the most dangerous ball-hawk in the NFL. He not only recorded nine interceptions in 2004, but he also ran them back for an incredible total of 358 yards.

Baltimore's Ray Lewis (number 52) speaks to Ed on the sidelines. Ed credited Lewis, one of the best linebackers in the NFL, with helping him to become a better defensive player.

Nobody in the 70-year history of the league had ever covered more ground in one season after picking off passes.

When the 2004 season ended, there could be no doubt who would win NFL Defensive Player of the Year. Ed Reed became the first safety in 20 years to earn this honor, which made winning the award even more special.

Ed now had something in common with his close friend and teammate Ray Lewis, who had won the award in 2003. Ed was thrilled to be mentioned in the same breath as Lewis, who has been considered one of the greatest linebackers in history. Soon after winning the award, Ed gave his buddy some of the credit:

> **The fact that Ray and I trained together and talked abut it and knowing that you can get to this level on discipline and focus, he pretty much walked me to it. He was giving up his time to me. There are certain things he taught me. . . . For me to achieve the award and him to have done it already, it's truly an honor to be among such great names that achieved this before our time.**

Ed was no longer a player with only the potential to be great. In just three years, he was already considered one of the best safeties to ever grace an NFL field.

CROSS-CURRENTS

Read "Defensive Player of the Year" to learn about the honor that was awarded to Ed after the 2004 season. Go to page 51. ▶▶

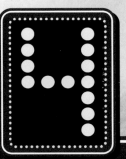

BETTER PLAYER AND BETTER MAN

When a tragic event occurs in the world, it often makes the game of football seem unimportant. Hurricane Katrina was one such tragic event. This disastrous storm hit in August 2005, and it struck an area that was very dear to Ed Reed. It devastated his home state of Louisiana and badly damaged his hometown of St. Rose.

Ed knew that as a professional football player earning millions of dollars, he could help the victims of Hurricane Katrina. He understood that as a famous athlete, he could raise money to help rebuild what had been destroyed.

Ed still had to concentrate on football, but as he prepared for the season in Baltimore, his heart was in Louisiana.

Ed was preparing for the 2005 football season when he heard that Hurricane Katrina had devastated his hometown. He immediately decided to put his fame to use helping people left homeless by the storm.

Hurricane Katrina left about 80 percent of New Orleans (pictured) flooded for several weeks. More than 1,800 people died as a result of the powerful storm. Katrina also caused an estimated $81.2 billion in damage in the southeastern United States.

Reaching Out

In early August 2005, Ed Reed and his Ravens had been in New Orleans to play an exhibition game against the Saints. The city was as beautiful and as vibrant as ever. Just a few days later, however, Hurricane Katrina hit New Orleans. Hundreds of people were killed, and thousands of homes were destroyed. Many of the people who survived no longer had a place to live.

Ed's hometown of St. Rose had also been badly damaged during the storm. Ed felt he needed to help the people in and near his hometown, and so he did just that. He created a hurricane relief fund through the American Red Cross.

That wasn't all Ed did. Ed and teammate Deion Sanders called upon every NFL player to donate $1,000 or more to the relief effort. Ed spoke with passion about what Katrina had left in its wake:

CROSS-CURRENTS

To learn about the career of a great defensive back who teamed up with Ed in 2004, read "Deion Sanders." Go to page 52. ▶▶

> **❝It hurts us to talk about it. We know how bad it is in New Orleans, Alabama, and Mississippi. These families don't have things to eat. Me being from down there, I know it's a lot worse than what we see on television. . . . People see dead bodies around. It's horrific.❞**

Giving Back

Ed's concern was hardly surprising. He had always felt the need to help others, not only in his hometown but also in Baltimore and its surrounding areas.

Ed often spoke to students at Baltimore area schools, and he gave tickets to Ravens games to those students who worked hard in the classroom. Ed provided 40 needy families with Thanksgiving turkeys in 2005, and he helped feed the homeless on that same holiday in 2006. He also became involved with the Police Athletic League, a group that helps disadvantaged youth stay active in sports.

Such selfless acts only scratch the surface of Ed's community work. He also holds a football camp every summer at Destrehan High School. He even convinced other NFL stars, including Ray Lewis, to join him. Ed sent a message to the hundreds of kids who participated:

" Surround yourself with positive people. You have positive role models all around you in your coaches and your teachers. There's always going to be someone saying something negative about you or to you. But you've got to keep going. You've got to look up. **"**

Ed needed to take his own advice during the 2005 season. It was a season of physical and mental challenges for the star safety. For the first time in his professional career, Ed would be forced to watch from the sidelines as his teammates played. When he finally returned to action, he wasn't the same ball-hawk that had driven quarterbacks and wide receivers crazy.

Put to the Test

Ed felt fine as the 2005 season approached. He had no reason to worry. He was settling into the prime of his career. Remarkably, he had intercepted at least one pass in half of the games he had played in during the previous two seasons.

By his fourth season, Ed was among the most respected and even feared players in the NFL. Coaches had tried in vain to draw up game plans that would keep him from hurting their teams. Receivers had tried in vain to beat him consistently. All had failed. They were forced to simply avoid the area of the field where Ed was likely to be. He seemed, however, to be everywhere.

CROSS-CURRENTS

For some history about the National Football League franchise that Ed plays for, read "The Baltimore Ravens." Go to page 52. ▶▶

Among those who marveled at Ed's talent and instinct for the game was Indianapolis Colts **tight end** Marcus Pollard. Pollard wished that the defensive backs on his team could intercept as many passes as Ed did:

" He's a very special guy. [Ed] can hit you, and then he can cover you. I make fun of our defensive backs that they can't catch the ball, otherwise they'd be playing wide receiver. This is a guy that has great hands, and then he has the ability to return [the interceptions]. **"**

Ed signs autographs during a break at the Ravens' training camp, 2005. After finishing 9-7 in 2004, the team had expected to improve in 2005. However, the Ravens' offense struggled to score points, and Baltimore lost most of its games.

Some might have said Ed was due for an off year. Others believed only an injury could have prevented him from maintaining his usual excellence. In any case, he simply didn't perform as well from the moment the first football was kicked in 2005.

Whatever ailed Ed seemed to be catching. The same Ravens that had enjoyed winning seasons in 2003 and 2004 lost seven of their first nine games in 2005. Ed, the man who a year before had been the most prolific pass thief in the NFL, went game after game without recording an interception.

Injured

On October 16, 2005, Ed's season went from bad to worse. During the fourth quarter of a game against Cleveland, he suffered an ankle injury. He knew this injury would put him out of action for a while.

Ed walking on the field during a 2005 home game. Without Ed in the starting lineup, the Ravens lost five of six games that year. When he did play, Ed was only able to intercept one pass. However, the star safety did knock down nine other passes in 10 games.

The injury left Ed frustrated. He was used to playing football every week. He wanted desperately to come to the aid of his team, which certainly needed him that season, but he couldn't help. Ed was forced to just watch as the Ravens continued to lose.

While Ed was sidelined, the Ravens lost five of six games. The team's usually dominant defense collapsed, giving up 24 points a game during his absence, including an unheard-of 42 in a loss to Cincinnati.

Ed's importance to the team was displayed upon his return. It was apparent that he was rusty when he returned from his injury. He even dropped a few potential interceptions, which was not like him. However, the Ravens won three of their next four games, including an impressive 48-3 victory over the Green Bay Packers. At that point, however, the team's playoff chances were gone, and the Ravens were playing only for pride. Ed recorded his only interception of the season in the final game against Cleveland.

Such a terrible season both for Ed and the team would not—*could* not—happen again. Everyone in a Ravens uniform—and especially the safety who wore number 20—would make certain of that.

A Big Contract

Everyone needs to feel appreciated—even the biggest sports stars in the world. Ed Reed is no different. On July 7, 2006, the Ravens did something that made Ed feel very appreciated. They offered him a contract that would keep him with the team for the next seven years.

The deal was for $40 million, including a $15 million bonus just for signing the contract. Ed was about to become an extremely rich man. After the 2006 season, Ed would have been able to offer his talent to any team in the NFL, but he decided to sign the contract and remain in Baltimore. That brought a smile to the face of Ravens **general manager** Ozzie Newsome. Newsome was relieved that Ed would be staying with the team:

> **He knows he is going to be here for the long-term now and be part of the plans in the big picture. And he can devote his energies now to football matters and to being the playmaker he has always been for us.**

Some athletes lose the motivation to work hard after they sign huge contracts. Ed, however, vowed that he would never lose his motivation. He thought about his father, who would rise before dawn to go to his job every day. That work ethic was ingrained in Ed at a very young age. When asked about his $40 million contract, Ed spoke humbly:

> **Money doesn't define me. It never did. It never will. I'm a football player, and I go ahead with that. We need certain things to survive. That's just something that added more to me. It's a blessing, first and foremost. I thank the Ravens for that.**

Back to Form

The Ravens would soon be thankful as well. In 2006, Ed's fifth season, he immediately showed that he was back to his brilliant self. In the first game of the season, he intercepted a pass and helped his team shut out Tampa Bay, 27-0.

More importantly, Ed played a key role in making the Ravens the biggest comeback team of the year. The team won its first four games, lost the next two, and then won five more in a row to raise its record to 9-2. By midseason, Ed was really on a roll. He recorded another interception in a win against the Tennessee Titans and added two more in a victory over the Kansas City Chiefs in early December.

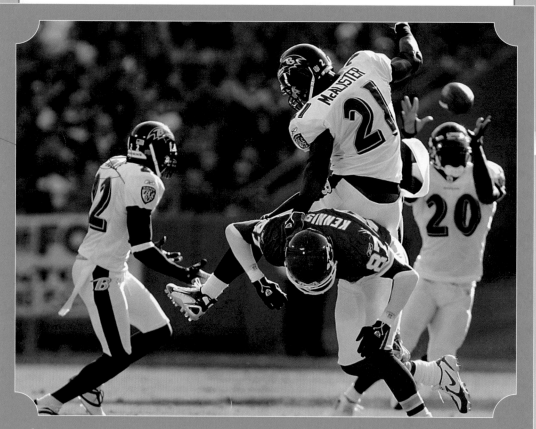

Ed prepares to grab a pass intended for Kansas City wide receiver Eddie Kennison (number 87), December 10, 2006. Ed picked off two passes and knocked down three others in Baltimore's 20-10 victory over the Chiefs.

That Ravens' victory marked the beginning of a four-game winning streak to end the regular season, and Baltimore earned a playoff spot. Ed finished the regular season with three interceptions in the last four games, including one he ran back 37 yards in a 31-7 triumph over the Pittsburgh Steelers.

When the playoffs began, Ed was certainly ready. He intercepted two passes against Indianapolis quarterback Peyton Manning, who was considered the best at his position in the NFL. The Ravens defense stifled and frustrated Manning and the explosive Colts, but the offense didn't play as well. The Ravens suffered a 15-6 loss that ended their season.

Ed went home for the winter, but he and his fellow Ravens wished they had advanced to the Super Bowl, the dream of every team. Even though those dreams were dashed, Ed knew that he had justified his team's faith in him when it offered him one of the biggest contracts ever given to an NFL safety.

Ed was still one of the best defensive backs in the league. That definitely wouldn't change in 2007.

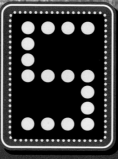

GENEROUS HEART AND SURE HANDS

Ed Reed always understood that he had an obligation to his team, his fans, and himself to perform to the best of his ability. As time passed, however, Ed gained a greater understanding of another obligation he felt he had. He believed he should serve as a role model for children.

Some athletes believe kids should look to their parents and teachers for guidance. Ed, however, feels that children inevitably will also be influenced by the lives of football players. As he moved forward in his career, Ed wanted to make certain he was setting a good example.

Returning to His Roots

Setting a good example meant much more to Ed than just showing

Ed takes a break from practice to sign an autograph for a fan. The star safety has spoken about the importance of being a good role model both on and off the field.

a good work ethic on the field and avoiding trouble off the field. He wanted to get personally involved in improving the lives of others.

Ed was particularly committed to the youth of Baltimore and to the children who grew up in his hometown of St. Rose, Louisiana. After Hurricane Katrina hit Louisiana, Ed wanted even more to help the children there.

Hurricane Katrina struck in 2005, but rebuilding the most damaged areas could not be done quickly. Ed knew the rebuilding could take years. In May 2007, he launched a golf tournament to raise money to help people in the hurricane-affected areas as well as needy families in Baltimore.

CROSS-CURRENTS

To learn more about the devastation caused by Hurricane Katrina in August 2005, read "Storm of the Century." Go to page 54.

Such an endeavor came as no surprise to anyone. Over the years, Ed had donated his own money to Destrehan High School and to several charities through the Ed Reed Eye of the Hurricane Foundation. Just days before Ed unveiled plans for the golf event, he announced that his foundation had provided college **scholarships** to three Destrehan High School students.

The golf event would aid many people in need, but Ed was quick to point out that his main concerns were the children of Baltimore and his devastated hometown. He knew his talent gave him the opportunity to help others. He spoke about that with passion:

> **"It's all for the kids. I didn't have that when I was growing up, you know, athletes in the neighborhood doing things. I just didn't see it. Football is my heart. I wouldn't be here without it. And we need to do whatever we can do to better their future and help them get ahead in life."**

A young fan talks to Ed Reed during a paintball competition organized to raise money for charity. Ed donates his time and money to many good causes. Most of Ed's charitable work helps young people.

Among the projects Ed believed would help children was the construction of playgrounds in the St. Rose area. Such work was funded by money coming out of Ed's own pocket as well as by contributions from large companies. The golf outing, however, would open the door for anyone to become a sponsor.

Ed knew that life was more than just football. To many in the United States, especially those affected by Hurricane Katrina, affording a place to live or buying food for the dinner table was a daily struggle. Ed also understood, however, that without football, he wouldn't have been in a position to help others.

What made it easier for Ed was that he loved to play the sport. In 2007, despite his team's struggles, Ed played football well enough to earn yet another trip to the Pro Bowl in Hawaii.

Preparing for the Season

The blazing sun beat down on the Baltimore Ravens in training camp as they prepared for the 2007 season. The players and coaches were motivated by their success in 2006, but they also were driven to advance further into the playoffs.

On August 1, 2007, Ed showed up at camp wearing a black T-shirt that read, "What's higher than No. 1?" His question referred to the Ravens' defense, which had ranked first in the NFL the previous year.

Ed's message was that the defense could still improve. In fact, he was already thinking about ways to make it better. One of those ways was to avoid long pass plays against him and his fellow defensive backs. Although the Ravens had led the NFL with 28 interceptions in 2006, they had also given up 20 pass plays of 30 yards or more.

Ed blamed himself as much as anyone. In one game against the Carolina Panthers, he had failed to cover a receiver on a long pass that resulted in a 72-yard touchdown. It proved to be a key play in the Ravens' only loss in Baltimore all season.

Ed believed that communication was the key to cutting down the number of big plays against the defensive backs. As the leader of those defensive backs, he felt it was his job to speak up:

❝We have a lot of things we can get better on, and communication is definitely one that you have to stay

up on. Those are the small things that we messed up on last year—when we gave up touchdowns that we shouldn't have given up.**

Off to a Good Start

Early in the 2007 season, there was no reason to believe the Ravens hadn't taken the momentum from 2006 and run with it. They opened the season with a loss at Cincinnati, but they won four of their next five games. The defense, which had been shaky to start the year, came together. The Ravens gave up just 10 points combined in games against the San Francisco 49ers and St. Louis Rams. The defensive backs intercepted five passes against St. Louis.

After Baltimore reached the playoffs in 2006, expectations were high for the 2007 team. Ed came into the team's training camp focused on improving the Ravens' defense. Here, he brings down a teammate during practice.

Ed played well in 2007. He intercepted seven passes and knocked down 13 others. He also returned punts on occasion, including one 63-yard touchdown return. However, after a 4-2 start, the Ravens lost nine straight games.

By that point in the season, Ed was really on a roll. He had recorded an interception in three consecutive games and had run for at least 15 yards with each of the interceptions. He was on pace to break his personal record of nine interceptions in a season.

CROSS-CURRENTS

Check out "The Ravens' Rivals" to learn about two of the team's most bitter opponents, the Browns and the Steelers. Go to page 54. ▶▶

Then, suddenly, the Ravens and their defense seemed to fall apart. The team lost nine games in a row and fell hopelessly out of the playoff race. In six of those games, the Ravens defense gave up 27 points or more.

Ed was among the only bright spots in what became a dismal season. He intercepted three more passes during the Ravens' losing streak. He often covered huge chunks of the field by himself, which amazed fellow players and coaches, including Bill Belichick of the undefeated New England Patriots. In an interview just before the two teams played early in December, Belichick expressed high praise for the veteran safety:

"To me, when he's in the deep part of the field, it's hard to throw in the deep part of the field with him being back there. . . . He's a tremendous playmaker. Not only does he come up with a lot of balls, but, as we've seen, when he has it in his hands he's a threat to score. . . . He's a tremendous football player."

A Tough Loss

When the Patriots and Ravens met for a Monday Night Football game on December 3, 2007, it seemed to be a mismatch. The Patriots had a win-loss record of 11-0, and they had already beaten some of the best teams in the NFL. They also had the highest-scoring offense in the NFL, thanks to star quarterback Tom Brady and receivers like Randy Moss, Donté Stallworth, and Wes Welker. The Ravens, meanwhile, were struggling with a record of 4-7. Many people believed Baltimore would lose by three touchdowns to the Patriots.

The Ravens, however, rose to the challenge. Brady and his teammates struggled against the Baltimore defense. Near the end of the first half, Brady tried to complete a pass to Welker. The ball bounced off Welker's hands, and Ed grabbed it. He turned upfield and ran for the Patriots' end zone. He was tackled after a 32-yard return, and, unfortunately, he lost control of the ball during the tackle. The Patriots recovered Ed's fumble on their own 25-yard line, but they decided not to try another play before halftime.

Overall, Ed played well during the game. He helped hold the speedy Moss to just four catches for 32 yards—well below the receiver's season averages. The Ravens game also marked the first time all season that Tom Brady had been held in check. Brady managed to complete just 18 of his 38 passes for 257 yards. In the end, however, the Patriots managed to escape with a 27-24 win to remain undefeated.

Ed reaches for a tipped ball during the 2007 game between Baltimore and Indianapolis. Although the Ravens had played well against unbeaten New England, the next week the team came back to earth with a 44-20 loss to the Colts.

Wearing an AFC jersey, Ed Reed laughs during practice before the Pro Bowl, February 2008. Ed is a fan favorite because of his ability on the field, as well as his desire to improve both his team and his community.

For Ed and the Ravens, the close loss to the NFL's premier team was another disappointment in the 2007 season. Baltimore finished that year with a 5-11 record, last in the AFC's North Division. Statistically, however, Ed had a pretty good year, pulling down seven interceptions.

A Look into the Future

Ed Reed has always believed that his personal acomplishments on the field mean very little if his team does not succeed. Like most players, his goal is to win the Super Bowl. He has said that a victory in the NFL's biggest game would make his career complete.

Ed has become a celebrity because of his on-field success. Unlike some other famous athletes, however, Ed has refused to allow his celebrity status to change his personality. He believes that fame should be used to help the lives of others. Throughout his NFL career, Ed has continued to help people in need, especially children. He has also achieved his goals without placing the spotlight on himself.

Only time will tell just how much Ed will accomplish as a player. He did not turn 30 until September 11, 2008, so he is still relatively young. Unlike running backs or linemen, who take a beating on every play, defensive backs often enjoy long careers.

Ed began making his mark on the record books from the moment he stepped onto an NFL field. He recorded 34 interceptions in his first six seasons, setting a Baltimore team record. At this rate, Ed is on pace to become one of the top ten players in the league for interceptions by his 36th birthday. Among modern players, only Washington's Champ Bailey had intercepted more passes by age 30.

Nobody knows for sure just what Ed Reed will accomplish before he finally hangs up his cleats. One thing is clear—the children of Baltimore, Maryland, and St. Rose, Louisiana, will continue to benefit from Ed's fame and fortune for many years to come.

The Pro Bowl

The idea to gather the best players in the NFL at the end of the year for an all-star game first came about in 1938. The game, however, didn't become an annual event until 1951. This game was known as the Pro All-Star Game until 1970, when the American Football League (AFL) merged with the National Football League. It was then renamed the Pro Bowl.

The Pro Bowl is played every year in February, one week after the Super Bowl, the game that determines the NFL champion. Since 1980, the Pro Bowl has been held at Aloha Stadium in Honolulu, Hawaii, which ensures a warm climate and an enjoyable experience for the fans as well as the players and their families.

Until 1995, the Pro Bowl participants were chosen by a vote of NFL players and coaches. Since that time, the fans have been given the chance to help select players. The votes of the fans, players, and coaches are all weighed equally in determining who will represent the AFC and NFC in the game. All voters are expected to choose the players who have enjoyed the best seasons.

The Pro Bowl does not feature the rough play of a regular season game. It is generally more of a fun game than a competitive experience for the players. The players' goals are not only to win the game, but also to prevent getting injured or injuring others. The intensity of the play typically doesn't pick up until the fourth quarter, when the game's outcome hangs in the balance.

The game often features wide-open offenses and a great deal of passing, which makes it more enjoyable for both the fans in the stadium and the people watching at home on television. The teams usually score many touchdowns. Since 2000, the winning Pro Bowl team has tallied 31 points or more in eight of the nine games.

Though the players on the winning team receive a little more money for their efforts, the outcome of the game is not considered very important to most participants and fans. Neither the NFC nor the AFC has proven dominant in the Pro Bowl for a long period of time. Since 1981, neither conference's team has ever won more than three games in a row.

Immediately following each Pro Bowl, the player determined to have performed the best in the game is presented with the Most Valuable Player award. Every player, however, feels honored to have been chosen to play with the top talent in the NFL. (Go back to page 6.) ◀◀

A Safety Issue

NFL fans often enjoy debating who the premier player is at various positions. Though many believe Ed Reed is the best safety in the league, others might argue that this distinction belongs to Troy Polamalu of the Pittsburgh Steelers or to John Lynch of the Denver Broncos.

Polamalu became famous not only for his great talent but also for his long curly hair that runs well down his back. He is considered the "new kid on the block" among great safeties. He established himself quickly with the Steelers, earning a starting position in his second season, and he has been voted into the Pro Bowl every year since 2005.

Former Steelers coach Bill Cowher compared Ed Reed and Polamalu in glowing terms:

> **"**One thing about both of these players, they're both very instinctive. They have great instincts and a great feel for the game. That's what separates them from other safeties.**"**

Of this trio of AFC all-stars, John Lynch is the veteran. He began his career in 1993 with the Tampa Bay Buccaneers and became a mainstay on one of the best defensive teams in the NFL. He joined the Broncos in 2004 and earned a trip to the Pro Bowl in each of the next four years. Lynch is among the all-time leaders in Pro Bowl appearances, playing nine times during his brilliant career. (Go back to page 6.) ◀◀

Safety Troy Polamalu of the Pittsburgh Steelers entered the NFL a year after Ed Reed. Polamalu is considered by many to be one of the best safeties in the American Football Conference.

All about St. Rose

In Louisiana, you usually have to drive quite a while to get from the state's many small towns to a big city.

That's not the case with St. Rose, Louisiana. After a short trip north on Route 626 and a quick turn east on Route 61, you're in New Orleans, which is not only Louisiana's largest city but also one of the most interesting and entertaining places in the United States.

St. Rose lies near the southeastern corner of the state. People who enjoy warm weather can appreciate its location. The average temperature throughout the winter is 50° Fahrenheit (10° Celsius), but it consistently reaches 90°F (32°C) in summer. Heavy rains in the early summer months do tend to cool things off, and the area is often threatened during hurricane season.

Unlike nearby New Orleans, which is known for its jazz music and nightlife, St. Rose is a fairly quiet town with a population of about 7,000.

Fortunately for the people of St. Rose, the cost of living in the area is rather low compared to the national average. You must spend much more money, however, to enjoy the activities in New Orleans, which is one of the more expensive cities in the United States. (Go back to page 11.) ◀◀

The Miami Hurricanes

These Hurricanes are not the ones that have devastated Louisiana over the years. They are the ones that have devastated opposing college football teams. They are the University of Miami Hurricanes in Miami, Florida, the team on which Ed Reed played.

The Hurricanes compete in the Coastal Division of the Atlantic Coast Conference (ACC), which also boasts such football powers as Florida State, Georgia Tech, and Boston College. Since 1937, the Hurricanes played all of their home games at Orange Bowl Stadium. Starting in 2008, however, they began sharing Dolphin Stadium with the NFL's Miami Dolphins.

The history of Miami Hurricanes football began in 1927. The team had some success in the late 1930s and 1940s, and then again in the 1950s, but it was not considered among the nation's elite until Howard Schnellenberger became the coach in 1979. Schnellenberger's teams won 41 of 57 games and earned Miami's first national title.

Since the early 1980s, the 'Canes, as they are affectionately known to their fans, have been one of the most dominant teams in the country. They have competed well enough to earn a spot in a postseason bowl game 23 times in the last 27 years. Only teams that win most of their games are invited to participate in bowl games.

Over the years, the Hurricanes have won some of the most prestigious bowl games in the country. They captured nine Big East Conference titles from 1991 to 2003 before joining

When Ed was a member of the Hurricanes, the team played its home game at the Miami Orange Bowl. The university's logo can be seen in the center of the field in this aerial view of the stadium.

the ACC in 2004. They even won national championships in 1983, 1987, 1989, 1991, and 2001.

Miami's program has produced a number of great NFL players. **Wide receiver** Reggie Wayne and running back Edgerrin James, both of whom helped make the Indianapolis Colts a dominant team, wore Miami Hurricane uniforms. NFL stars such as running back Willis McGahee and wide receiver Santana Moss also played for the Hurricanes.

Former professional football greats such as quarterback Bernie Kosar, running back Ottis Anderson, offensive lineman Jim Otto, and defensive linemen Ted Hendricks and Warren Sapp played for Miami as well.

The legendary coach Jimmy Johnson and his successor Dennis Erickson coached during Miami's most dominant era, from 1984 through 1994. The Hurricanes won three national championships during that stretch.

The team hasn't been quite as successful since then, but it is still among the best in the country. Nearly every season it produces players who make their marks in the NFL. (Go back to page 15.) ◀◀

The Great Ray Lewis

Quarterbacks and running backs have become just a little more nervous before games against the Baltimore Ravens, and Ray Lewis is the reason why.

Ray is one of the most feared defensive players ever. In 2003, this linebacker became only the sixth player in league history to be named the NFL Defensive Player of the Year twice. He has been selected to the AFC Pro Bowl team eight times.

Born in Bartow, Florida, in 1975, Ray first displayed his talent at Kathleen High School, where he registered an amazing total of 207 tackles and eight interceptions as a senior. He also ran three of those interceptions back for touchdowns and achieved 10 sacks, which are recorded when a defensive player tackles a quarterback behind the point where the ball is snapped. Ray even recovered five fumbles that year. In 2007, he was selected by the Florida High School Athletic Association to be on its All-Century Team, placing him among the top 33 high school football players in state history.

Ray was a versatile athlete during his high school days. He also won the 1993 state wrestling championship in the 189-pound weight division.

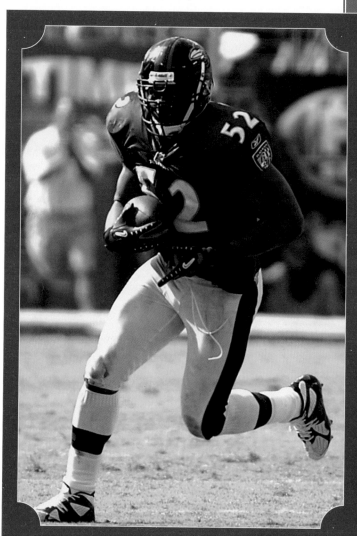

Ed's teammate Ray Lewis is considered one of the best linebackers in NFL history. Unfortunately, legal troubles off the field—including his link to a murder case in 2000—have at times overshadowed Lewis's career accomplishments and charitable work.

His high school performance, however, was only the beginning of his athletic greatness. Ray went on to play at the University of Miami, where, as a sophomore and junior, he led the entire Big East Conference in tackles.

The Ravens chose Ray in the first round of the 1995 draft. He soon earned a reputation as a complete defender. He uses his speed and relentless attitude to track down quarterbacks attempting to throw the ball and running backs trying to carry it. He is also one of the best linebackers in the NFL at intercepting passes.

Though aggressive and a little bit mean on the field, Ray has a giving heart. He started the Ray Lewis 52 Foundation to raise money and provide help for children in the Baltimore area. His charitable work has included adopting ten families during the holidays and helping them make their Christmas dreams come true. He has also sponsored a food drive during Thanksgiving to help feed hungry people.

Ray even learned to speak Portuguese and Amharic to better help African children who have been devastated by war and famine. He traveled to Angola and Ethiopia to deliver wheelchairs and crutches to disabled people in those countries. (Go back to page 19.) ◀◀

Defensive Player of the Year

The NFL consists of 32 teams. Each team is allowed to have 53 players. That's 1,096 players in all. Among the more than 500 who play defense, only one player can be the NFL Defensive Player of the Year.

Indeed, only the best players in the league have earned the honor, which is presented at the end of each season. Usually this award goes to a linebacker or a defensive lineman, mainly because these players are involved in every play, whether the ball is run or passed.

The award was launched in 1971 and is given by the Associated Press. This award was created to give more attention to defensive players, who don't receive as much publicity as offensive players such as quarterbacks, running backs, and receivers.

The only three-time winner of the NFL Defensive Player of the Year award is former New York Giants linebacker Lawrence Taylor. Many people believe Taylor was the greatest defensive player in history at any position. In fact, he even earned the Defensive Player of the Year honor as a rookie. Ed Reed's teammate Ray Lewis is one of only five players who have won the award twice. (Go back to page 25.) ◀◀

Deion Sanders

In 2004, the Ravens signed a defensive back whose ability and personality had been the talk of football for more than a decade. That defensive back was Deion Sanders.

Sanders not only claimed to be the best; he proved it on the field. That field wasn't limited to football. Sanders was also talented enough to play major league baseball for four different teams.

Sanders was known for being brash, but he displayed incredible talent for 14 seasons in the NFL. He was one of the fastest players in football history. Sanders intercepted 52 passes and returned nine of them for touchdowns. He was selected to every Pro Bowl but one from 1991 to 1999, and he was named NFL Defensive Player of the Year in 1994.

Coaches even used Sanders as a wide receiver, and he was among the greatest kick returners of all time. His combined total of 19 interception and kick returns for touchdowns stands as an NFL record.

Sanders was nicknamed "Prime Time" for his self-confidence and for his ability to perform at his best with victory or defeat hanging in the balance. Sanders also received attention for his unique dances in the end zone after he scored touchowns.

Following his retirement in 2005, Sanders began a new career as a television football commentator. He remains as outspoken as ever. (Go back to page 29.) ◀◀

The Baltimore Ravens

In the dark of night, on March 19, 1984, Baltimore Colts owner Robert Irsay ordered 15 transport vans to pick up all of his team's property. The vans transported the Colts' property to Indianapolis.

That night, the Indianapolis Colts were born, and the Baltimore Colts were no more.

The next day, Baltimore football fans learned they had lost their hometown team. Most fans were angry. Many cried. They had lived and died with the Colts for 31 years. They would now face Sunday afternoons with no football team for which to root.

Eleven years later, on November 6, 1995, those same fans who had cried were crying again, but now they were shedding tears of joy. On that day, Cleveland Browns owner Art Modell announced he was moving his team to Baltimore. A new team that would eventually be named the Ravens was born. This time it was Cleveland fans who cried foul at the removal of their beloved team. Eventually, it was announced that a new team, also called the Browns, would be formed in Cleveland in 1999.

On September 1, 1996, however, people in Baltimore were excited to watch the Ravens run onto the field for their first game. The new team beat the Oakland Raiders, 19-14. The Ravens, however, would only win three more times that year.

The Ravens play a home game at their stadium in Baltimore. The Ravens won the Super Bowl after the 2000 season. Since then, however, the team has not achieved the same level of playoff success.

The team's performance, however, gradually improved. The Ravens won just six games in both 1997 and 1998, but they finished 8-8 in 1999. The fans' optimism finally seemed justified.

In 2000, the Ravens blossomed. They won their last seven games of the regular season to qualify for the playoffs for the first time in team history. Rookie linebacker Ray Lewis anchored a defense that allowed only an amazing 10.3 points a game.

The Ravens were just getting started. The team surrendered just 16 points in three playoff games to reach the Super Bowl. Millions of Americans tuned in on television to the showdown that would determine the NFL champion. The Ravens easily defeated the New York Giants, 34-7. They had finished the season with an 11-game winning streak.

After that magical year, the Ravens continued to be one of the better teams in the league, especially on defense. They qualified for postseason play in 2001, 2003, and 2006, but they didn't win another playoff game after any of those seasons.

While many coaches come and go on NFL teams, the Ravens stuck with their coach through thick and thin. Brian Billick coached the team from 1998 to 2007 before John Harbaugh took over in 2008. (Go back to page 30.) ◀◀

Storm of the Century

The people of New Orleans and the entire Gulf Coast region of the United States were braced for a major hurricane in late August 2005. They had no idea, however, just how much damage this hurricane would cause.

Hurricane Katrina struck the United States on August 29. The storm and its resulting floods killed a total of 1,836 people, making Katrina the deadliest hurricane to hit the United States in 77 years. It was also the costliest natural disaster in U.S. history, causing an estimated $81.2 billion in damage.

The greatest loss of life and property occurred in New Orleans. The storm, along with poor protection against flooding, caused hundreds of deaths and the loss of thousands of homes. About 80 percent of the city reported flooding. The residents' misery was made worse by government relief efforts that have been criticized as slow and poorly planned.

The hurricane also laid waste to coastal Alabama and Mississippi. In Missisippi, flooding extended as far as six miles inland, and the cities of Biloxi and Gulfport were severely damaged.

Although much has been done to help the victims of Hurricane Katrina, the damage to the area and its people will be felt for years to come. (Go back to page 37.) ◀◀

The Ravens' Rivals

Football rivalries are built and maintained in a variety of ways. Some rivalries occur naturally, when teams are located near each other. Other rivalries are fostered by intense competition or specific events in a team's history.

The Baltimore Ravens have two fierce rivals: the Pittsburgh Steelers and the Cleveland Browns. The passion that exists among the fans of these two teams developed for two different reasons.

The rivalry between the Ravens and the Steelers developed mainly because the two teams have spent much of the last ten years battling for the division title. The rivalry between the Ravens and the Browns has a different source. Many Browns fans are still angry that their original team moved to Baltimore in 1995.

The Steelers were part of the NFL before the Browns entered the league in 1950. The Steelers struggled for decades before developing into one of the most successful teams in the league in the early 1970s. Great coaches such as Chuck Noll and Bill Cowher have graced the team's sidelines. Pro Football Hall of Fame players such as defensive lineman Joe Greene, linebacker Jack Lambert, quarterback Terry Bradshaw, and running back Jerome Bettis have helped Pittsburgh win five Super Bowls, including four of six from 1975 to 1980.

The Browns have yet to participate in a Super Bowl, but they, too, have had a rich history. They dominated the league during the first 15 years of their existence, winning four championships and playing in four other title games. The Browns were led by Hall of Fame players such as quarterback Otto Graham and Jim Brown, who is still considered by many to be the greatest running back in NFL history.

The Browns also have enjoyed some strong seasons since the Super Bowl was established in 1967. They made the playoffs a number of times. The Browns reached the AFC Championship game in 1986, 1987, and 1989, but lost all three years.

Tragedy for Browns fans struck in 1995 when owner Art Modell announced he was moving the team to Baltimore. The loyalty of Browns fans, however, saved football in Cleveland. Their outcry motivated the NFL to promise to place a new team in Cleveland if the city agreed to build a stadium. The stadium was completed in 1999. That year, the new Cleveland Browns were born—and so was the intense rivalry with the Baltimore Ravens. (Go back to page 42.) ◀◀

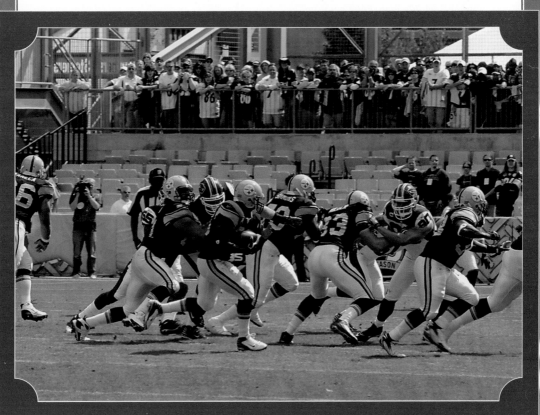

The Pittsburgh Steelers are one of the NFL's oldest franchises—this picture shows the team winning its 500th game in September 2007. The Steelers had a long rivalry with the Cleveland Browns, which continued when that franchise moved to Baltimore.

1978   Ed Reed is born on September 11 in St. Rose, Louisiana.

1995   Ed moves in with the family of his high school assistant principal's secretary, and Ed's motivation and grades improve markedly.

1996   Ed is selected District Defensive Most Valuable Player by the *New Orleans Times-Picayune*.

1997   Ed wins the state championship in the javelin throw for the Destrehan High School track team.

Ed enrolls at the University of Miami on a football scholarship.

2001   The *Football News* names Ed college football's Defensive Player of the Year.

Ed helps the University of Miami win a national championship.

2002   Ed is selected by the Baltimore Ravens as the 24th overall pick of the NFL draft.

Ed earns a starting spot and leads the team with five interceptions.

2003   After a strong season, Ed is selected for the Pro Bowl for the first time.

2004   Ed intercepts nine passes and is named the NFL Defensive Player of the Year.

Ed launches his annual football camp for children at Destrehan High School.

2005   Ed begins charitable work to relieve suffering in Louisiana after Hurricane Katrina.

2006   Ed signs a six-year contract extension with the Ravens worth $40 million.

2007   Ed intercepts seven passes during the 2007 season.

2008   Ed plays in the Pro Bowl for the fourth time.

Career Statistics

Year	Team	G	Total Tackles	Solo Tackles	Assisted Tackles	Int.	Yds.	TD
2002	Balt	16	85	71	14	5	167	0
2003	Balt	16	71	59	12	7	132	1
2004	Balt	16	76	62	14	9	358	1
2005	Balt	10	37	33	4	1	23	0
2006	Balt	16	59	51	8	5	70	1
2007	Balt	16	39	29	10	7	130	0
TOTAL		90	367	305	62	34	880	3

Team Records

2004 Most interceptions in a single season: 9
(NFL and team record) Longest interception return for a touchdown: 106 yards
(NFL and team record) Most yards gained after interceptions, season: 358 yards

2007 Most interceptions in a playoff game: 2

Awards and Championships

1997 *Times-Picayune* District Defensive Most Valuable Player
State champion in javelin throw

2000 First-team All-Big East Conference

2001 Big East Co-Defensive Player of the Year
Football News National Defensive Player of the Year

2003 NFL Pro Bowl

2004 NFL Defensive Player of the Year and NFL Pro Bowl

2006 NFL Pro Bowl

2007 NFL Pro Bowl

Books

Frager, Ray. *Storybook Season: The 2000 Baltimore Ravens' Run to the Super Bowl*. Baltimore: Baltimore Sun, 2001.

Matte, Tom. *Tom Matte's Tales from the Baltimore Ravens Sideline*. Champaign, IL: Sports Publishing, 2004.

Nichols, John. *The History of the Baltimore Ravens*. Mankato, MN: Creative Education, 2005.

Patterson, Ted. *Football in Baltimore: History and Memorabilia*. Baltimore: The Johns Hopkins University Press, 2000.

Steadman, John. *From Colts to Ravens: A Behind-the-Scenes Look at Baltimore Professional Football*. Centreville, MD: Tidewater Publishers, 1997.

Web Sites

http://www.baltimoreravens.com/

The official Web site of the Baltimore Ravens features team news, statistics, schedules and other information on the team.

http://www.nfl.com/players/edreed/profile?id=REE192451

This NFL site provides information about Ed Reed's professional career, including game logs, season statistics, and a personal profile.

http://sports.espn.go.com/nfl/player/content?statsId=5910

This ESPN Web site features news stories on Ed Reed throughout as well as statistical information on his career.

http://www.nfl.com

This is the official homepage of the National Football League.

http://pro-football-reference.com/

This Web site provides statistics on all National Football League teams and players.

All-American—the name given to a top college football player. This honor is awarded through a vote by members of the national news media in a process approved by the National Collegiate Athletic Association (NCAA).

All-Pro—a top NFL player in a particular year. Sportswriters who are members of the Associated Press pick the All-Pro players of each year.

American Football Conference (AFC)—one of the two conferences, or groups of teams, in the National Football League (NFL). The AFC grew out of the old American Football League (AFL), which competed with the NFL throughout the 1960s and merged with the NFL in 1970.

defensive back—a football player who is mainly responsible for covering receivers on pass plays. Defensive backs try to keep receivers from catching the ball.

defensive coordinator—a coach who is responsible for the overall performance and strategy of a team's defense.

draft—the process by which NFL teams select new team members from the nation's top college football players.

general manager—the administrator of a football team who is responsible for getting good players on a team by negotiating contracts with the players or trading players with other teams.

interception—the stealing of a pass, usually thrown by the quarterback, by a member of the opposing team's defense.

linebacker—one of three or four defensive players who line up behind the defensive linemen and are responsible for stopping offensive players on both runs and passes.

National Football Conference (NFC)—one of the two conferences, or groups of teams, in the National Football League (NFL). The NFC came into being when the NFL and American Football League (AFL) merged in 1970.

playoffs—a series of games played between the best football teams in a particular year to determine the players in that year's Super Bowl.

punt—the act of kicking the ball away to the opposing team after the offense has failed to keep possession of the ball.

recruit—to attempt to convince a top high school football player to attend a specific college and play for that college's team.

safety—a defensive back who either helps cover a receiver directly or plays a particular area of the field in an attempt to prevent passes from being completed.

scholarship—an award of money given to a person to pay all or a portion of the costs to attend college.

scout—a person who works for a specific team and looks for talented athletes to play on that team.

tight end—an offensive player generally responsible for either blocking or receiving passes.

training camp—the period in July and August in which NFL players and coaches prepare for the coming fall season.

wide receiver—one of several offensive players whose main task is to catch passes thrown by the quarterback.

page 6 "I have to be reminded . . . " Don Markus, "For Reed, Virtue of Patience Has Been His Biggest Reward," *Baltimore Sun* (January 9, 2007).

page 8 "Football is that up-and-down . . . " Markus, "For Reed, Virtue of Patience Has Been His Biggest Reward."

page 9 "I didn't want to throw . . . " Nick Abramo, "Romo Gets Over His Mistakes," *Honolulu Star-Bulletin* (February 11, 2007).

page 11 "Son, you don't ever want . . . " Jeffri Chadiha, "Look At Me Now," *Sports Illustrated* 103, no. 9 (September 5, 2005), p. 72

page 13 "There was something inside . . . " Chadiha, "Look At Me Now."

page 18 "I'm always thinking about football . . . Aaron Wilson, "Ravens' Reed Primed for Second Season," *Carroll County Times* (June 11, 2003).

page 19 "[Ed's] a guy who loves the game . . . " Wilson, "Ravens' Reed Primed for Second Season."

page 21 "After I [blocked the punt] . . . " Aaron Wilson, "Ravens' Reed is a 'Spectacular Player,'" *Carroll County Times* (October 13, 2003).

page 21 "Spectacular player . . . " Wilson, "Ravens' Reed is a 'Spectacular Player.'"

page 22 "It's really just exciting . . . " Associated Press, "First Safety in 20 Years to Win Defensive Award," ESPN.com (January 7, 2005). http://sports.espn.go.com/nfl/news/story/id=1961735

page 25 "The fact that Ray . . . " Aaron Wilson, "Ravens' Reed Wins NFL Defensive Player of the Year," *Carroll County Times* (January 7, 2005).

page 29 "It hurts us to talk . . . " "Deion Wants All Pros to Donate $1K to Katrina Relief," ESPN.com (September 3, 2005). http://www.sports.espn.go.com/espn/news/story?id=215006

page 30 "Surround yourself with positive people . . . " Eric LeBlanc, "Ed Reed Comes Home for the Kids," *St. Charles Herald* (July 7, 2004).

page 30 "He's a very special guy . . . " Barry Wilner, "Defensive Player of the Year: Ed Reed," *Football Digest* 34, no. 7 (April 2005), p. 32.

page 33 "He knows he is going . . . " Len Pasquarelli, "Ravens Lock Up Safety Reed with Six-year Extension," ESPN.com (June 27, 2006). http://sports.espn.go.com/nfl/news/story/id=2502163

page 33 "Money doesn't define me . . . " Aaron Wilson, "Top Free Safety in the Game," *Carroll County Times* (July 31, 2006).

page 38 "It's all for the kids . . . " Lori Lyons, "NFL Standout Gives at Home," *The Times-Picayune* (May 19, 2007).

page 39 "We have a lot . . . " Mike Duffy, "Secondary Works on Communication," Baltimoreravens.com (Aug. 2, 2007). http://www.baltimoreravens.com/News/Articles/2007/08/Secondary_Works_on_Communication.aspx

page 42 "To me, when he's in . . . " Erik Scalavino, "Getting a Reed on the Ravens," Patriots.com (November 28, 2007). http://www.patriots.com/news/index.cfm?ac=latestnewsdetail&pid=29301&pcid=41

page 47 "One thing about both . . . " Gerry Dulac, "Polamalu, Reed Are New Breed of Safety," *Pittsburgh Post-Gazette* (November 24, 2006).

American Football Conference (AFC), **5**, 6, 9, 46
Anderson, Ottis, 49

Bailey, Champ, 45
Baltimore Ravens, 16–25, 30–35, 39–45
 draft Reed, 15
 history of the, 52–53
 and the playoffs, 8, 21–22, 35
 and rivalries, 54–55
 See also Reed, Ed
Belichick, Bill, 42
Bettis, Jerome, 54
Billick, Brian, 21, 53
Bradshaw, Terry, 54
Brady, Tom, 42, 43
Brown, Jim, 55
Brunell, Mark, 23

charity work, 26–27, 29–30, 36–39, 45
Cleveland Browns, 22, 52, 54–55
Cowher, Bill, 47, 54

Defensive Player of the Month award, 23
Defensive Player of the Year award, 25, 50, 51
Destrehan High School, 10, **12**, 13, 15, 29, 38

Ed Reed Eye of the Hurricane Foundation, 38
 See also charity work
Erickson, Dennis, 49

Garcia, Jeff, 22
Graham, Otto, 55
Greene, Joe, 54

Hall, Jeanne, 10–13
Harbaugh, John, 53
Hendricks, Ted, 49
Hurricane Katrina, 26–29, 37, 39, 54

Irsay, Robert, 52

James, Edgerrin, 49
Johnson, Jimmy, 49

Kennison, Eddie, **34**
Kosar, Bernie, 49

Lambert, Jack, 54
Lewis, Ray, 22, **24**, 25, 29, 50–51, 53
Lynch, John, 47

Manning, Peyton, 35
Martin, Scott, 15
McGahee, Willis, 49
Miami Hurricanes, **14**, 15, 48–49
Modell, Art, 52, 55
Moss, Randy, 42, 43
Moss, Santana, 49

National Defensive Player of the Year *(Football News)*, 15
National Football Conference (NFC), 9, 46
Newsome, Ozzie, 33
Nolan, Mike, 19
Noll, Chuck, 54

Otto, Jim, 49

Pittsburgh Steelers, 54–55
Polamalu, Troy, 47
Police Athletic League, 29
 See also charity work
Pollard, Marcus, 30
Pro Bowl, 4–6, 8–9, 22, **44**, 46, 50

Reed, Ed
 awards and honors won by, 15, 21, 22, 23, 25
 birth and childhood, 10–11
 and charity work, 26–27, 29–30, 36–39, 45
 at Destrehan High School, 10, **12**, 13, 15
 and earnings, 33
 and education, 10, **11**, 12–13
 and injuries, 6, **7**, 31–32
 and interceptions, 6, 9, **14**, **17**, 18, 20–21, 22–23, 25, 30, 33, 34–35, **41**, 42–43, 45
 is drafted by the Ravens, 15
 and leadership, 39–40
 and the Pro Bowl, 4–6, 8–9, 22, **44**
 and punt coverage, 21–22
 records set by, 22
 rookie year, 16–20
 at the University of Miami, **14**, 15, 48–49
 See also Baltimore Ravens

Numbers in **bold italics** refer to captions.

Reed, Ed, Sr. (father), 11–12
Reed, Karen (mother), 11
Romo, Tony, 8–9

Sanders, Deion, 29, 52
Sapp, Warren, 49
Schnellenberger, Howard, 48

Special Teams Player of the
    Week award, 21
St. Rose, Louisiana, 10, 26,
    29, 37, 39, 45, 48
Stallworth, Donté, 42

Taylor, Lawrence, 51

University of Miami Hurri-
    canes, *14*, 15, 48–49

Watson, Kenny, *23*
Wayne, Reggie, 49
Welker, Wes, 42

Marty Gitlin is a freelance book writer and sportswriter based in Cleveland, Ohio. He has written more than a dozen books for students, including works on Brown v. the Board of Education and the Battle of The Little Bighorn and biographies of NASCAR drivers Jimmie Johnson and Jeff Gordon. Gitlin worked for two decades as a newspaper sportswriter, during which time he won more than 45 awards, including first place for general excellence from the Associated Press. The AP also selected Gitlin as one of the top four feature writers in Ohio.

PICTURE CREDITS